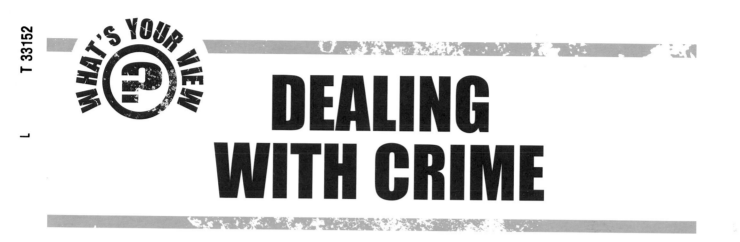

WHAT'S YOUR VIEW?

DEALING WITH CRIME

Judith Anderson

Smart Apple Media

First published in 2005 by Franklin Watts
96 Leonard Street, London EC2A 4XD

Franklin Watts Australia
45–51 Huntley Street, Alexandria NSW 2015

Series editor: Sarah Peutrill, **Art director:** Jonathan Hair, **Design:** Proof
Books, **Picture researcher:** Sophie Hartley

Picture and text credits: see page 48.

Note on Web sites:
Every effort has been made by the publishers to ensure that the Web sites
in this book contain no inappropriate or offensive material. However,
because of the nature of the Internet, it is impossible to guarantee that the
contents of these sites will not be altered. We strongly advise that Internet
access is supervised by a responsible adult.

Published in the United States by Smart Apple Media
2140 Howard Drive West, North Mankato, Minnesota 56003

Library of Congress Cataloging-in-Publication Data

Anderson, Judith.
Dealing with crime / by Judith Anderson.
p. cm. — (What's your view?)
Includes index.
ISBN-13 : 978-1-58340-972-5
1. Criminal justice, Administration of—Juvenile literature. I. Title. II. Series.

HV8693.A53 2006
364—dc22   2005054108

9 8 7 6 5 4 3 2 1

Contents

What's the issue?

A universal problem

Crime affects us all. Some experience crime first-hand, either as a victim, an offender, or perhaps a witness or police officer. We are all subject to the laws that define crime, and we all make choices about whether or not to break those laws. We are also influenced by fear of crime. Each time we lock our front door or avoid a "risky" part of town, we demonstrate the impact of crime on our society.

The criminal justice system

This book looks at how we deal with crime. It contains strong and often contradictory reactions because crime touches on some of our most basic rights as human beings—the right to life, the right to liberty, and the right to protect ourselves and our possessions. The task of the criminal justice system—including police, courts, and prison services—is to balance these rights so that the victim sees justice done, the innocent are protected, and the accused are tried fairly and without prejudice. It is a difficult task.

Statistics

The statistics used in this book reveal some of these problems. They are all "facts" of one sort or another, but they rarely present the whole truth. For example, identity theft is one of the fastest growing crimes in the U.S., but is this because more people are reporting it or because more people are committing it?

Yet statistics can reveal important trends and attitudes toward crime. They show, for example, that car theft is a common crime. They also show that methods of car theft are changing. Because car manufacturers are making new cars more secure, there is an increase of thieves breaking into homes to steal car keys.

Changing laws
The criminal justice system has to evolve in order to compete with changing attitudes and realities. The threat of terrorism, for instance, has shaped new laws and new police powers. Yet change should not come without debate. And at the heart of this debate lies what each of us believes is right and wrong.

Note on quotes
Quotes presented in this book in a specific context should not be understood to commit their source to one side of that debate. They are simply illustrations of the possible viewpoints in each debate.

Further information
Web sites for further information are given throughout the book. A good general Web site is www.usdoj.gov/kidspage/. This site is designed specifically for young people, providing information and advice about the law, crime, and the consequences of offending.

French police survey a beach—beaches are one of the most common places for crimes, especially theft, to occur.

Q: Is crime a greater problem today than it was 30 years ago?

MANY PEOPLE say that they are worried about rising crime. The evidence seems to be everywhere—in the media, on security cameras, and in overcrowded prisons. Yet the statistics on crime are not clear-cut. Variations in the type of crime, whether it is reported, and how it is recorded mean that comparisons with the past can be unreliable. However, some new types of crime have spread rapidly in the past 30 years, including "cyber crimes" such as identity theft and cell phone crime.

A young boy holds a sign protesting against violence in Venezuela. Several thousand people marched to protest against the government's failure to stop a wave of violent crime.

YES "Studies made in previous years predicted that by 1998, America would see a dramatic increase in crimes committed by juveniles. Well folks, we're beginning to see it! And it's not over yet."

Vic Bilson, conservative activist

"I've been mugged three times in the past two years—twice for my cell phone. Who says things are getting better? I don't feel nearly as safe as I did 10 years ago."

Irish mugging victim

"Data espionage and data theft, credit card fraud, child pornography, far-right extremism, and terrorists are ever more common on the Internet."

Joschka Fischer, German Foreign Minister

❊ STATISTICALLY SPEAKING

• In 2003, 73 percent of those questioned in a British crime survey said they believed crime was increasing. In fact, overall crime figures were down from the previous year by 3 percent, but violent crime was up by 2 percent.

NO "I haven't seen such continuous drops in so many categories of crime over such a long period."

Don Weatherburn, Director of the Bureau of Crime Statistics and Research, commenting on the third straight annual drop in crime in 2004 in New South Wales, Australia

✖ "The overall picture of crime in Canada looks very much like it did last year and the year before that. . . . It does not support claims by some people that Canada is becoming a more violent place."

Criminologist Rosemary Gartner, University of Toronto, Canada

✖ "The only real crime trend is increasing crime coverage. Between 1990 and 1995, there was a 240 percent increase in network news coverage of murders, even though the Justice Department reported that there was a 13 percent decline in homicides in that period."

Vincent Schiraldi, Director of the Justice Policy Institute

✱ STATISTICALLY SPEAKING

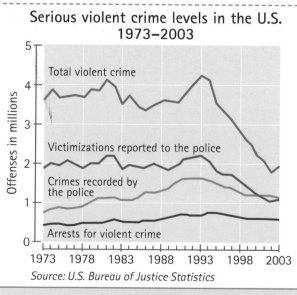

Serious violent crime levels in the U.S. 1973–2003

Total violent crime

Victimizations reported to the police

Crimes recorded by the police

Arrests for violent crime

Offenses in millions

Source: U.S. Bureau of Justice Statistics

CONFLICTING EVIDENCE?

"Britain continues to be one of the safest places in the world to live."

U.K. Home Office press release, 2001

Percentage of people who were victims of violent assault, robbery, car theft, or burglary once or more in one year:

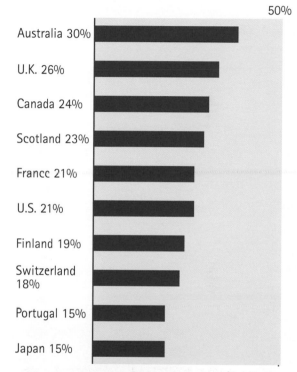

Australia 30%	
U.K. 26%	
Canada 24%	
Scotland 23%	
France 21%	
U.S. 21%	
Finland 19%	
Switzerland 18%	
Portugal 15%	
Japan 15%	

50%

Source: International Crime Victims Survey

MORE TO THINK ABOUT

The U.S. Bureau of Justice Statistics reported that 25 percent of violent crimes in 2003 occurred at or near the victim's home. Of all of the violent crimes reported that year, 53 percent of the incidents occurred during the day, between 6 a.m. and 6 p.m.

Q: Is deprivation an excuse for crime?

A homeless woman in Russia. Increasing poverty and homelessness have been linked to high crime rates in Russia.

LINKS BETWEEN deprivation (extreme poverty) and crime have been accepted for many years. However, such links do not prove that deprivation is a cause of crime, nor that it is an excuse. Many would argue that a starving child who steals food should not be treated as a criminal. But what about the teenager who commits arson because he was excluded from school or the woman who shoplifts because she is unemployed and depressed?

✔ **YES** "Gary Graham's life is a testament to the unacceptable price society pays for . . . generational poverty, racial prejudice, sub-standard schools, job discrimination. . . ."
Richard Burr, lawyer for Gary Graham, a black American executed for murder

✔ "We worked with one young woman who had become involved in prostitution, and subsequently drug abuse, at the age of 13 because . . . her mom introduced her to various men so that the family could afford to eat."
Daljeet Dagon, Streetwork Team, Scotland

✔ "You don't have to probe very far into the backgrounds of children who wind up in police stations and courtrooms to find a common denominator: poverty."
Lisbet Palme, UNICEF

"I am sick of social deprivation being used as an excuse to justify crime. It's insulting. My parents were hard up and living in public housing when my sister and I grew up, but you don't see us out mugging, stealing, and vandalizing."

Dan, BBC Online "Have Your Say"

"Poverty may provide the environment for some crime, but it should not provide an excuse. Greed and selfishness are also principal causes."

Pastoral letter from the Catholic bishops of New Zealand

"As great as my compassion is for Robert Harris the child, I cannot excuse nor forgive the choice made by Robert Harris the man."

California Governor Pete Wilson's response to an appeal for Robert Harris, who murdered two teenagers. Robert Harris suffered physical abuse throughout his childhood.

✱ STATISTICALLY SPEAKING

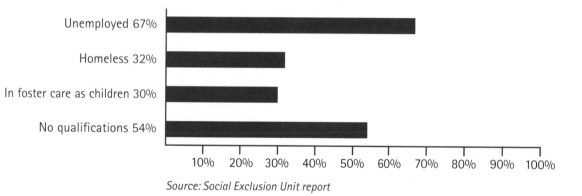
Levels of deprivation among the U.K. prison population, before their sentence

Unemployed 67%
Homeless 32%
In foster care as children 30%
No qualifications 54%

Source: Social Exclusion Unit report

CASE STUDY

RACHEL'S STORY
Rachel was rejected by her mother when she was seven years old. She lived in four different children's homes and ran away when she was 16. She had no money and was "befriended" by a drug addict. Within a week, she was taking drugs herself, and soon began stealing to pay for her habit. Two years later, she began a prison sentence for theft and shoplifting offenses.

MORE TO THINK ABOUT
While many deprived areas have high crime rates, some deprived areas have very low crime rates. These areas are typified by long-established communities in rural or semi-rural areas. The highest crime rates occur in areas of inner-city deprivation. What reasons might there be for this?

FIND OUT MORE: www.crime.org www.socialexclusion.gov.uk www.smartjustice.org

Q: Do we need more police on the streets?

MANY PEOPLE believe that more police with a more visible presence in the local community leads to less crime. They point to community policing initiatives where a "zero-tolerance" approach to minor offenses such as vandalism may have contributed to a recent drop in overall crime. However, some argue that too many police can increase conflict within communities. Others point out that putting more police on the streets may mean fewer police working on "hidden" crimes such as fraud or child abuse.

�֍ STATISTICALLY SPEAKING

• A poll conducted in the U.K. found that 70 percent of those asked said that more police on the streets would make them feel safer in their area.

YES

"American research has shown that one of the most effective uses of police resources is high visibility at crime hotspots. . . . In Australia, the number of police has failed to keep pace with the escalating crime rate for the past 40 years."

Nicole Billante, The Center for Independent Studies, Australia

✓ "We have had a lot of trouble with children down by the shops being abusive. Every now and then, the police come around to check that everything is okay, but they should do it more often."

Maureen Brookes, resident of a quiet suburb

✓ "The key to creating a safer community is a greater police presence."

Sarah Teather, Liberal Democrat Member of Parliament, U.K.

✓ "Put more police on the streets, and they'll catch more criminals. It's not rocket science, is it?"

Conservative Party campaign poster, U.K.

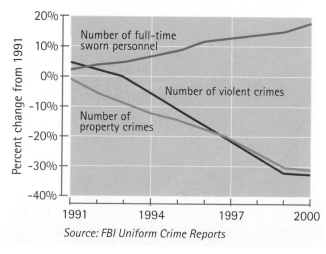

A large police presence at a biotechnology protest in San Francisco. Are large numbers of police at protests necessary?

CONFLICTING EVIDENCE?

Washington, D.C., had 631 police officers per 100,000 population in 2000—the highest ratio of police in the U.S. It also had one of the highest murder rates, and, between 1990 and 2000, the percentage of crimes solved in Washington dropped from 57 percent to 36 percent.

Source: The Washington Post

Percentage change in number of crimes and number of full-time police officers in large cities in the U.S. between 1990 and 2000:

Percent change from 1991

- 20%
- 10% — Number of full-time sworn personnel
- 0%
- −10% — Number of violent crimes
- −20% — Number of property crimes
- −30%
- −40%

1991   1994   1997   2000

Source: FBI Uniform Crime Reports

NO

"It is very difficult to see a direct connection between increasing numbers of police officers and automatically solving one particular area of crime."

Zaki Hashmi, British criminal lawyer

❌ "Zero tolerance is nothing more than old-fashioned law and order along with the traditional over-policing of poor and marginal social groups."

Tim Anderson, New South Wales Council for Civil Liberties, Australia

❌ "Giuliani = Police State"
Message chalked on the street by Robert Lederman in protest of Mayor Rudolph Giuliani's police "crackdown" on crime in New York

MORE TO THINK ABOUT
It might be argued that police numbers themselves have little effect on crime; what matters is effective policing. What do you think is the most important aspect of a police officer's job?

FIND OUT MORE: www.nyc.gov/html/nypd   www.fbi.gov
www.popcenter.org   www.liberty-human-rights.org.uk

Q: Are prison sentences a crime deterrent?

THE EFFECTIVENESS of prison as a deterrent is controversial. Some argue that the more likely a criminal is to be imprisoned, the greater the deterrent. Others argue that it is the length of the sentence that counts. However, many ex-prisoners go on to re-offend, and some say that the experience of prison encourages crime. The type of crime also matters. Drug addicts and those who commit violent crimes may be less likely to consider the risk of prison before offending.

 NO

"Over 60 percent of the people inside are just kids, and we are just making them anti-society, anti-good."

Stephen P. Bohrer, former inmate of the California prison system

✖ "Many of these offenders have chronic problems related to drug use. . . . There are very few formal mechanisms available for such offenders to be linked to community-based services upon release. . . . Therefore, the drug and crime cycle is regularly perpetuated."

South Australia Department of Correctional Services

✖ "Potential offenders don't seriously take into account getting caught, so it doesn't matter what you're threatening to punish at the other end."

Professor Paul Robinson, University of Pennsylvania

❋ STATISTICALLY SPEAKING

• In the U.K., more than 50 percent of all prisoners discharged are reconvicted within two years of their release. For young male offenders, the reconviction rate is about 75 percent. In South Australia, 80 percent of all prisoners discharged in 2001 had a prior history of imprisonment.

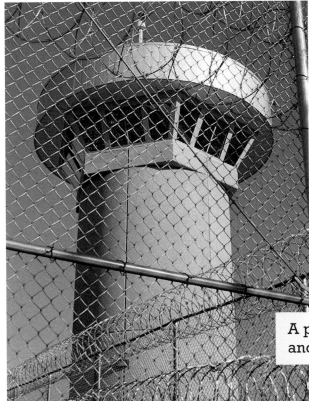

A prison in Colorado for repeat and high-profile offenders.

YES

"Spain imprisons four times more people than Scotland, relative to recorded crime, and Ireland three times more. Unsurprisingly, the deterrent is such that crimes per capita in both Ireland and Spain is around a quarter of the level in Scotland."

Annabel Goldie, Member of the Scottish Parliament

✓ "The prospect of prison, more than any other sanction, is feared by white-collar criminals and has a powerful deterrent effect."

U.S. Deputy Attorney General Larry Thompson

✓ "A Home Office report in 2000 found the average offender carried out 140 offenses per year. . . . If we were to jail 5,000 criminals who would otherwise have committed 140 offenses, then 700,000 offenses against the public would be prevented by 12 months in jail."

David Green, Director of the U.K. Institute for the Study of Civil Society

CASE STUDY

A YOUNG OFFENDER'S STORY

Levi is an 18-year-old offender. He has been involved in crime since his early teens.

"I am 18, with two children, who I love and adore very much, but, yet again, I am in [prison] for a robbery, which was stupid to do. I have been in nearly seven months. . . . Let me just say one thing: crime is not worth the hassle of being separated from your loved ones. You might have heard this before, but I have learned my lesson. I can guarantee [prison] will not see me again."

✱ STATISTICALLY SPEAKING

Burglary rates and incarceration rates in the U.S. and U.K.

Number of burglaries per 1,000 households

Number of incarcerated burglars per 1,000 alleged burglars

Source: International Crime Victim Survey

MORE TO THINK ABOUT

In some prisons, as many as four out of five inmates have some kind of psychological disorder. Does mental illness reduce the effectiveness of prison as a deterrent to crime?

Q: Should ID cards be introduced to tackle crime?

IDENTIFICATION (ID) cards are intended to prove we are who we say we are. ID cards show details such as the holder's name, address, age, benefit entitlements, and, in some countries, religion or ethnicity. They often include a photograph and may even hold "biometric" data, such as iris scans or fingerprints, to discourage forgery. Many argue that ID cards can help tackle crime, terrorism, and illegal immigration. However, issues of cost, confidentiality, and abuse have deterred countries such as the U.S. and Australia from introducing them.

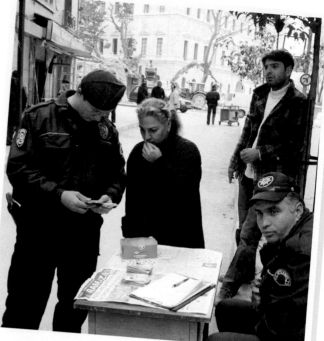

A Turkish police officer returns an ID card to a Turkish woman at a checkpoint set up after a series of terrorist attacks in Istanbul in 2000. Suicide bombers killed over 50 people and injured many more.

YES

"A national ID card plan will provide a 'gold standard' for . . . protecting individuals from the modern-day crime of identity theft, protecting public services for use by those who are properly entitled to them, and helping us tackle crime, terrorism, and illegal immigration and working."

David Blunkett, former British Home Secretary

✓ "ID cards are vital in the fight against crime, as they enable officers to identify suspects quickly and thereby inconvenience individuals less."

Jan Berry, Chair of the Police Federation of England and Wales

✓ "Australia really needs to get serious about a national ID card based on biometric data . . . reliance on non-biometric-based documents such as passports and drivers' licenses is an invitation to conduct ID fraud."

Clive Williams, director of terrorism studies, Australian National University

✸ STATISTICALLY SPEAKING

• A poll taken shortly after the September 11, 2001, terrorist attacks showed that 68 percent of Americans favored a national identity card "to bolster anti-terrorism concerns."

14

CONFLICTING EVIDENCE?

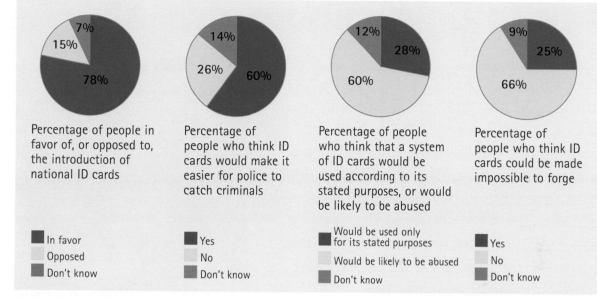

Percentage of people in favor of, or opposed to, the introduction of national ID cards

- In favor
- Opposed
- Don't know

Percentage of people who think ID cards would make it easier for police to catch criminals

- Yes
- No
- Don't know

Percentage of people who think that a system of ID cards would be used according to its stated purposes, or would be likely to be abused

- Would be used only for its stated purposes
- Would be likely to be abused
- Don't know

Percentage of people who think ID cards could be made impossible to forge

- Yes
- No
- Don't know

Source: UK YouGov Survey

NO

"A national ID card will not prevent terrorism. It would not have thwarted the September 11 hijackers, for example, many of whom reportedly had identification documents on them and were in the country legally."

American Civil Liberties Union

✗ "No form of documentation is totally secure and 'unforgeable'. If one (legitimate) person has the technology to make an ID card, then another (illegitimate) person can have it, too."

Adrian Beck, Lecturer in Security Management, University of Leicester, U.K.

✗ "The success of ID cards as a means of fighting crime or illegal immigration will depend on a discriminatory checking procedure which will target minorities."

Simon Davies, Director General of Privacy International

MORE TO THINK ABOUT

This debate raises many issues that have not been covered here. They include: confidentiality, cost, whether children as well as adults should have ID cards, and whether they should be mandatory or voluntary.

Mark Oaten, a British politician, says, "It would be better spending money on the police than a piece of plastic." What do you think?

FIND OUT MORE: www.privacy.org www.liberty-human-rights.org.uk
www.identitycards.gov.uk www.dmv.org

Q: Is the death penalty the best way to fight serious crime?

MANY COUNTRIES around the world have abolished the death penalty (capital punishment), but two of the biggest, the U.S. and China, still use it. Most supporters of the death penalty do not believe it should be used for all murders, only for the worst crimes, such as child murder or premeditated murder. However, those who oppose its use say that it is immoral, is an ineffective deterrent, and can lead to the execution of innocent people.

Katerina Koneva was murdered by Andrezej Kunowski, "the beast of Poland." He had been released from prison after similar offenses. Exercising the death penalty earlier would have prevented her murder.

YES

"Any crime which the law regards as serious should certainly receive serious penalties, and any crime which is punishable by the death penalty according to the law should certainly receive the death penalty."

Hu Jintao, President of the People's Republic of China

✓ "We have no hate or bitterness in our hearts. But that doesn't mean he does not pay for his crime."

Vikki Haack, after witnessing the execution of her sister's killer

✓ "If we execute murderers and there is in fact no deterrent effect, we have killed a bunch of murderers. If we fail to execute murderers, and doing so would in fact have deterred other murders, we have allowed the killing of a bunch of innocent victims. I would much rather risk the former."

John McAdams, Marquette University

✿ STATISTICALLY SPEAKING

• Of the approximately 1,000 prisoners executed in the U.S. between 1976 and 2005, not one has been retroactively proven innocent.

NO

"Amnesty International opposes capital punishment. . . . Its effectiveness as a unique deterrent to crime has never been proven, and with levels of crime continuing to rise in China, its irrelevance to crime control and prevention cannot be ignored."

Amnesty International

✗ "Capital punishment in my view achieved nothing except revenge."

Albert Pierrepoint, hangman in the U.K. for 25 years

✗ "Errors can and have been made repeatedly in the trial of death penalty cases."

U.S. Congress Subcommittee on Civil and Constitutional Rights

CONFLICTING EVIDENCE?

"Each execution results, on average, in 18 fewer murders—with a margin of error of plus or minus 10."

Emory University

✻ STATISTICALLY SPEAKING

• Between 1973 and 2004, 117 people from 25 states were released from death row because of evidence of wrongful conviction.

• A comprehensive study found that the death penalty costs North Carolina $2.16 million more per execution than a non-death penalty murder case with a sentence of life imprisonment.

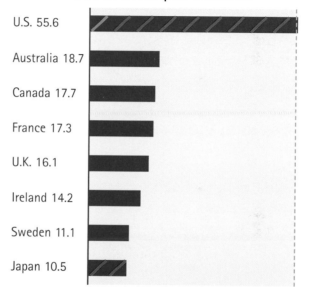

Murders in developed countries

U.S. 55.6	
Australia 18.7	
Canada 17.7	
France 17.3	
U.K. 16.1	
Ireland 14.2	
Sweden 11.1	
Japan 10.5	

countries with the death penalty Number of homicides per million people (average per year, 1999–2001)

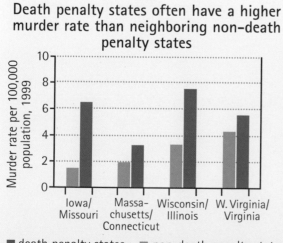

Death penalty states often have a higher murder rate than neighboring non-death penalty states

Murder rate per 100,000 population, 1999

Iowa/Missouri — Massachusetts/Connecticut — Wisconsin/Illinois — W. Virginia/Virginia

■ death penalty states ■ non-death penalty states

MORE TO THINK ABOUT

There are lots of key issues about the death penalty. This page covers cost, retribution, innocence, victims, morality, and deterrence, but there are other issues that can be considered: for example, mental illness, race, and religious viewpoints.

FIND OUT MORE: www.amnesty.org www.deathpenaltyinfo.org
www.prodeathpenalty.com www.dpinfo.com www.mvfr.org

Q: Should prisons be used for treatment rather than punishment?

WHAT ARE prisons for? Most countries agree that punishment, deterrence, and rehabilitation all play a part. The hope is that when prisoners are released, they have not only paid for their crimes, but they are somehow "reformed" and will not re-offend. Studies show that training and treatment can reduce re-offending rates, but some argue that the only way to protect society from violent criminals is to lock them up indefinitely.

YES

"We know from long experience that if [former prisoners] can't find work, or a home, or help, they are much more likely to commit more crimes and return to prison. . . . America is the land of the second chance, and when the gates of the prison open, the path ahead should lead to a better life."
George W. Bush, U.S. President

"It's self-evident in terms of value for money that if we can get people off drugs, on to [reform] programs, and into education, then we're going to reduce crime."
Martin Narey, Director-General of U.K. Prison Service

"The treatment of persons sentenced to imprisonment shall have as its purpose to establish in them the will to lead law-abiding and self-supporting lives after their release and to fit them to do so."
United Nations High Commission for Human Rights

CASE STUDY

THE "MOORS MURDERESS"

Myra Hindley was sentenced to 25 years in prison for her role in the murders of five children in the U.K. in 1956. Her crimes were horrific, but the judge at her trial recommended a limit on her sentence because he believed she had the potential for reform.

During her years in prison, she studied for a degree, turned to Christianity, and reputedly showed remorse for her crimes. The parole board decided that she no longer represented a threat to society and recommended her release. Nevertheless, public opinion was strongly opposed to Hindley's freedom, and successive Home Office ministers used their powers to extend her sentence for an indefinite period. She died in prison in 2002.

NO

"Prison should be a form of punishment, not a vacation or a place where murderers can get a degree in psychology at the taxpayers' expense."

P. Olohan, BBC Online "Talking Point"

✖ "There are crimes so heinous that we must draw a line in the sand. We must say to criminals, 'if you commit one of these crimes, you are finished. You don't get a second chance.'"

Matt Salmon, Arizona State Representative, speaking in favor of the "No Second Chances for Murderers, Rapists, or Child Molesters" bill

✖ "What do we do with [sex offenders]? We keep them away from children at whatever cost. If it means incarcerating them forever, so be it. Don't allow them to be back out among children again."

Wendy Utting, Australian child protection advocate

❖ STATISTICALLY SPEAKING

• In 1996, 6 percent of U.S. prison budgets were spent on rehabilitation programs, and 94 percent were for building, staffing, and maintaining prisons.

❖ STATISTICALLY SPEAKING

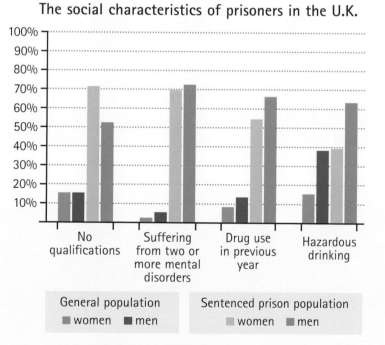

The social characteristics of prisoners in the U.K.

General population: ■ women ■ men
Sentenced prison population: ■ women ■ men

Source: Social Exclusion Unit Report

MORE TO THINK ABOUT

Other points to consider are:

Should drug addicts and the mentally ill be in prison in the first place?

What is the cost to society of treatment and education programs?

Should release from prison be conditional on participation in a rehabilitation program?

FIND OUT MORE: www.aclu.org   www.bop.gov
www.hmprisonservice.gov.uk   www.prisonreformtrust.org.uk

Q: Is trial by jury the fairest way to reach a verdict?

MANY PEOPLE believe that juries underpin the basic right to a fair trial. While their use differs from country to country, the central principle is that the defendant is judged by a group of his or her peers, so that the verdict is both fair and free from government interference. Nevertheless, some issues can cast doubt on the fairness of jury trials, including corruption, intimidation, prejudice, and whether jurors are able to understand complex evidence, especially in trials involving fraud or technology.

YES

"In all criminal prosecutions, the accused shall enjoy the right to a speedy and public trial, by an impartial jury of the State and district wherein the crime shall have been committed."

U.S. Constitution: Sixth Amendment

✓ "Give me a jury any day rather than a case-hardened judge on nodding terms with the police."

Helena Kennedy, British civil liberties lawyer

✓ "The research shows that while certain elements of complex trials do tax jurors' comprehension and understanding, there is no firm evidence that their judgments have therefore been wrong. Jurors are capable of solving highly complex cases."

Robert D. Myers, U.S. judge

NO

"Our proposals for trial by judge alone address the problems in trying a very small number of fraud and complex financial cases. Such trials can last for months on end. They make it difficult to find a representative jury. . . . Evidence must be pared down, and charges against the defendant reduced, in order to make trials manageable. This cannot be right."

Lord Falconer, British Minister of State for criminal justice, sentencing, and law reform

✗ "In practice . . . juries are massively swayed by one or two vocal individuals. There is also a strong pressure to conform to a unanimous verdict."

Professor Richard Dawkins, Oxford University, U.K.

✗ "In a high-profile case like this, and the media grabs hold of it, the evidence has to be so overwhelming before an individual is charged with a case that I personally kind of lean toward his guilt before we even get started."

A potential juror's comments during a selection interview at the trial of Theodore Kaczynski, who was found guilty of carrying out a series of deadly bombings

CONFLICTING EVIDENCE?

"All persons selected for jury service shall be selected at random."

Superior Court of California

- - - - - - - - - - - - - - - ⬇ - - - - - - - - - - - - - - -

In California in 1995, black ex-football player O.J. Simpson went on trial for murder. The selection of jurors was tainted by accusations of racial bias from both sides.

Composition of the initial jury pool

17%
15%
28%
40%

Composition of the final jury selected

75%
8%
17%

Composition of California's population in 1995

7.7%   34.3%
                (other = 0.6%)
57.4%

- white
- African American
- Hispanic
- Asian
- other

O.J. Simpson (center) was acquitted of murder in a widely criticized trial.

✴STATISTICALLY SPEAKING

- In a New Zealand study, trial judges said they would have reached a verdict different from the jury's in 24 out of 48 cases. In most cases, the disagreement was over the credibility of key witnesses. In 6 of the 48 cases, jurors said that "feeling time was running out" or that "people wanted to get home" were factors in reaching a verdict.

MORE TO THINK ABOUT

In some countries, and in some kinds of trial, a verdict does not have to be unanimous. A majority verdict often prevents a trial from collapsing without a verdict, and it can help to prevent undue pressure being placed on jurors who disagree. However, a majority verdict means that there is some doubt in one or more jurors' minds. Which is fairer?

FIND OUT MORE: www.crfc.org/americanjury www.courts.sa.gov.au
www.juror.cjsonline.org www.uscourts.gov

Q: Is it every adult's right to own a gun?

OWNING A gun means different things to different people. Hunters and farmers say that guns are essential to their way of life. Others use guns for other forms of sport. Many people think that they should be allowed to own a gun to defend themselves and their property. They argue that this works as a deterrent to crime. However, anti-gun activists believe that gun ownership increases gun-related crimes, and that anti-gun laws are essential to protect people from such violence.

Women who behave passively when attacked are 2.5 times more likely to be seriously injured than women who have a gun when confronted by a criminal, according to Professor John Lott, author of *More Guns Less Crime.*

YES

✓ "A person must have the right to defend his or her life from violence. The right to self-defense is meaningless unless you are able to defend yourself in an effective manner. Thus, the right to have arms is . . . an expression of the right to life."

Karen MacNutt, contributing editor, Women & Guns

✓ "A well-regulated Militia being necessary to the security of a free state, the right of people to keep and bear Arms shall not be infringed."

Second Amendment, U.S. Constitution

✓ "Firearm registration and owner licensing threatens long-standing Canadian liberties and freedoms. The type of gun control Canada has enacted is not consistent with many democratic principles."

Gary A. Mauser, The Fraser Institute, Canada

✷ STATISTICALLY SPEAKING

• Thirty-six percent of Canadians believe that members of the general public should be allowed to own a gun, and 87 percent believe that hunters and trapshooters should be allowed to own a gun. Of these, more than 90 percent favored a mandatory training course, a police background check, and a minimum age of 18 for anyone owning a gun. A majority also favored a psychological evaluation.

Gallup poll

CONFLICTING EVIDENCE?

The U.S. has a far more tolerant approach to gun ownership than the U.K. and Australia. Over 35 U.S. states have passed "right-to-carry" laws enabling licensed gun owners to carry a concealed firearm.

"Right-to-carry states have lower violent crime rates on average: 24 percent lower total violent crime, 22 percent lower murder, 37 percent lower robbery, and 20 percent lower aggravated assault. The five states with the lowest violent crime rates are right-to-carry states."

National Rifle Association of America

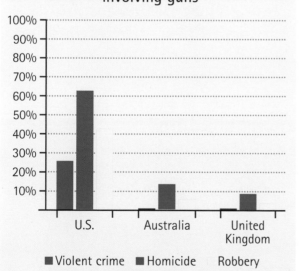

An international comparison of the percentage of violent crimes involving guns

■ Violent crime ■ Homicide Robbery

1998–2000 homicide rates per 100,000 population:

U.S. — 5.9
Australia — 1.9
U.K. — 1.7

"Ordinary citizens should not have weapons. We do not want the American disease imported into Australia."

John Howard, Australian Prime Minister

✗ "If future legislation falls short of a complete ban on handguns, let all of us be very clear about what we are being told. It says that we and our children are expendable so that 57,000 target shooters can retain their right to pursue a sport that uses weapons designed to kill."

Anne Pearston, campaigning for a ban on handguns in the U.K. after the shooting of 16 children and their teacher

✗ "We believe that the availability and lethality of guns make death or severe injury more likely in domestic violence, criminal activity, suicide attempts, and unintentional shootings."

Belief statement from U.S. gun-control organization the Million Mom March

❋ STATISTICALLY SPEAKING

• Approximately 45 percent of all U.S. households have firearms.
• According to gun-control groups, a British citizen is 50 times less likely to be a victim of gun homicide than an American.

MORE TO THINK ABOUT

This debate has been about the legal ownership of guns. However, most of the world's gun-related crime involves illegal weapons that have been stolen or imported without a license.

FIND OUT MORE: www.gun-control-network.org www.keepandbeararms.com
www.nra.org www.guncontrol.org.au

Q: Should children be treated as adults for serious crimes?

Should juvenile offenders be "named and shamed," or should their identities be protected by the courts?

IN MANY countries, and for most minor offenses, children can be tried in juvenile courts, where their vulnerability and immaturity may be taken into account. Yet juvenile courts are often seen as more lenient than adult courts. Some people believe this is not appropriate for repeat offenders and children convicted of violent crimes. They believe adult courts and long-term sentences should be used. But have a few well-publicized cases inflamed public opinion, or is the juvenile system really failing to protect society from delinquent children?

YES

"This could mean a 17-year-old being sent to the Children's Panel* for beating up his wife. . . . Delaying effective punishment sends out the wrong message and invites higher crime rates."

James Douglas-Hamilton, spokesman for the Scottish Conservative Party, commenting about a proposal for Children's Panels to deal with 16- and 17-year-old offenders

* A Children's Panel is a group of unpaid trained volunteers who decide whether mandatory measures of supervision are needed for the child, and, if so, what they should be.

✓ "If they commit the crime, they should receive adult time."
Grant McNally, Canadian Alliance MP

✓ "We MUST make serious juvenile offenders responsible as adults, according to their violent crimes."
Jeanette Basl, "Fed Up With Crime Committee"

❋ STATISTICALLY SPEAKING

• Twenty-three U.S. states set no minimum age at which children can be tried as adults.

NO

"When I first came to the court, everybody was talking about the 'juvenile super-predators,' so I kept waiting on the super-predators. They never came. What I saw were 14- and 15-year-olds scared to death."

Judge David A. Young, Baltimore City

✖ "Youths differ from adults in their knowledge and experience, time perspective, attitudes toward risk, understanding of alternatives and consequences, and susceptibility to peer-group influences."

Professor Barry C. Feld, University of Minnesota Law School

✖ "Glib slogans like 'Adult time for adult crime' betray the very people that society has failed and encourage 'warehousing' of juveniles—in prisons that in reality serve as training grounds for criminals."

Lisbet Palme, UNICEF

✺ STATISTICALLY SPEAKING

• In a study in Florida, children convicted in the adult system were compared by crime and background to children convicted in the juvenile system. It was found that while 30 percent of children prosecuted in the adult system were re-arrested within 2 years, only 19 percent of children in the juvenile system were re-arrested.

CASE STUDY

THE JAMIE BULGER CASE

In 1993, two 10-year-old boys, Robert Thompson and John Venables, were sentenced to a minimum of eight years in a young offenders institution for the murder of two-year-old Jamie Bulger. One juror at the boys' trial later said the verdict should have been "guilty as frightened and largely unaware children who made a terrible mistake and are now in urgent need of psychiatric and social help." The victim's mother said eight years was "too soon for what they have done".

MORE TO THINK ABOUT

The age of criminal responsibility is the minimum age at which a person can be charged with criminal actions. In India, Ireland, Switzerland, Thailand, and most U.S. states, this is age 7. In the United Kingdom it is 10, Italy and Germany 14, Spain 16, and Luxembourg 18. What age do you think it should be? Why?

FIND OUT MORE: www.buildingblocksforyouth.org/issues www.ncjj.org
www.youth-justice-board.gov.uk www.lawstuff.org.au

25

Q: Does community service work better than boot camps?

COMMUNITY SERVICE is sometimes used as an alternative to prison for less serious crimes. The offender must do supervised, unpaid work in the community for a set number of hours. Boot camps became popular in the U.S. in the 1980s and 1990s. The offender is sentenced to three or four months in a military-style camp with strict discipline and physical training. However, many argue that it is the elements of education and treatment at such camps that do the most to prevent re-offending.

NO

"If they are doing community service, say painting someone's fence, they could be staking the place out, thinking, 'When I've done my community service, I will go back there and do that house.'"

Lisa Stevens, U.K. burglary victim speaking on the BBC "Today" program

✖ "We should take 12- to 15-year-olds out of the neighborhoods in which they are causing the problem and into secure training. . . . You send out the message to the person's peer group that you don't come back laughing from the courts."

Ann Widdecombe, British Member of Parliament

✖ "Kids can't be coddled by the do-gooders of today; it doesn't do them any good. They have to learn discipline. And if they don't learn to fend for themselves, they've had it."

Ron Lovelock, who spent two years in a secure home for delinquent boys in the 1960s

YES

"Doing unpaid labor for 240 hours or any significant number of hours is a deprivation of liberty and is a serious punishment."

British judge Lord Bingham's view of community service in the U.K.

✔ "The bullying style and aggressive interactions that characterize the boot camp environment fail to model the pro-social behavior and development of empathy that these youth really need to learn."

U.S. National Mental Health Association

✔ "Community sentences aren't about being nice to offenders, they actually work. Offenders must be made to face up to their crimes and pay back to their communities for the harm they have caused."

Lucie Russell, Director of Smart Justice

A shock program for inmates at a prison in Florida.

Sample regime at a young offender institution

6:00 Rise, clean room, drill

6:40 Room inspection

7:20 Drill

8:00 Breakfast

8:30 Skills training, education

12:00 Lunch

1:00 Physical education

2:15 Skills training, education

4:45 Personal hygiene

5:00 Evening meal

6:00 Drama, art, drug awareness

8:00 Group meeting

8:30 Earned privileges

9:45 Personal hygiene

✱ STATISTICALLY SPEAKING

Victims of Crime survey
Percentage of victims preferring a community service sentence for young repeat-offending burglars

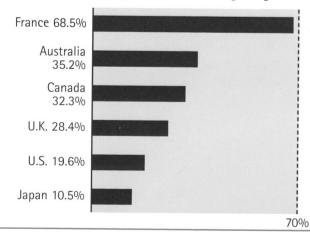

France 68.5%

Australia 35.2%

Canada 32.3%

U.K. 28.4%

U.S. 19.6%

Japan 10.5%

70%

✱ STATISTICALLY SPEAKING

• Re-offending rates at U.S. boot camps average between 64 percent and 75 percent. This is close to the re-offending rates at traditional correctional institutions.

MORE TO THINK ABOUT
"Community service" was officially renamed "community punishment" in the U.K. in 2002. Why do you think the government decided on this change of title?

Q: Are police doing enough to reduce car crime?

Some people say car crime is "victimless" because insurance companies pay for most of the loss. However, car owners have to pay higher insurance to cover the cost.

CAR CRIME is one of the most common types of crime. It includes vandalism, theft from a car, or theft of the car itself. A high proportion of offenders are either young "joy-riders" or opportunistic thieves who see an unlocked door or a purse on a car seat. They often commit multiple offenses before they are caught. Police initiatives tend to focus on raising public awareness about basic car security and catching the professional car thief who steals a car for re-sale or parts.

YES ✓ "It must be remembered that the responsibility lies with users and owners to reduce the risk of crimes being committed on their cars."
Department of Police and Public Safety, Tasmania, Australia

✓ "Car crime is a policing priority. [We use] a mixture of intelligence-led policing, pro-active work, and forensic analysis to catch and convict car thieves."
Essex Police reporting the launch of the U.K.'s first "decoy car"

✓ "Car thieves should watch out. We are constantly receiving information on their activities, and we will target anyone we believe is active in this type of crime."
Detective Inspector Kevin Mills, Sheffield, U.K.

✓ "I think [joy-riding] is a community problem. . . . I'd ask the community what they are doing about it and ask the parents what are their responsibilities."
Acting Assistant Commissioner Bob Hastings of the Melbourne Police, commenting after a joy-riding incident involving ten teenagers

NO

"Car crime has reached epidemic levels in Northern Ireland. Both the police and the courts could begin by taking a more strident line . . . in sentencing those so-called 'joy-riders' who frequently deal in death on our roads."

William McCrea, Democratic Unionist spokesman, Northern Ireland

✗ "I have watched as youths stole my neighbor's car in broad daylight—when I phoned the police, they said it was a 'low priority' incident."

Participant in the BBC Online "Talking Point"

✗ "Over the past few years, a proportion of police resources once allocated to fight vehicle theft has been reallocated to fighting crimes against the person. Because most stolen vehicles are replaced by insurance, the crime of vehicle theft is often perceived to be a 'victimless' one."

Insurance Bureau of Canada

✳ STATISTICALLY SPEAKING

• According to the Australian Institute of Criminology, the average car thief steals a car 47 times before being convicted.
• Forty-five percent of victims of car crime report incidents to the police, but just 1 in 10 expect anyone to be charged, according to one 2004 survey.

(Autoglass *Cracking Crime* Report)

MORE TO THINK ABOUT

Only about 14 percent of car thefts result in arrests in the U.S. The FBI says this is because of "the nature of the crime, its volume, and the degree of difficulty in solving this particular crime." Do they have a point?

Leaving your vehicle's engine running when nobody is in it is illegal in Pennsylvania. The idea is to deter opportunistic car thieves. But is it fair to vehicle owners?

FIND OUT MORE: www.racfoundation.org www.auto-theft.info
www.crimereduction.gov.uk/toolkits www.carsafe.com.au

Q: Do violent video games lead to violent crimes?

The overwhelming majority of children who play "first person shooter" games do not commit violent acts.

MANY PEOPLE believe instinctively that "first person shooter" games, in which the player participates in graphic screen violence, lead to increased aggression. Studies show that such games lead to short-term increases in aggressive activity among young children, but the evidence for older children and adults is less clear. Some argue that violent games can actually reduce violent tendencies by releasing aggression in a harmless way.

✔ "These games send kids the message that violence is acceptable, exciting, and without consequence."

Mary Lou Dickerson, U.S. State Representative and mother of two

✔ "We are raising the risk that more people will be inclined to use violence when put into a conflict situation, and they're more likely to become desensitized to the use of violence by other people."

Barbara Biggins, Young Media Australia

✔ **YES** "High levels of violent video game exposure have been linked to delinquency, fighting at school, and violent criminal behavior."

Professor Craig Anderson, Iowa State University

• People in the U.S. and Japan have arguably similar rates of participation in violent video games. Yet Japan's murder rate is around 800 per year in a population of 127 million, while in New York, the murder rate is around 600 per year in a population of just 8 million.

CASE STUDY

WARREN LEBLANC

Warren Leblanc, 17, murdered 14-year-old Stefan Pakeerah after luring him to a park. Stefan's family believes that Leblanc was acting out an adult-rated video game called *Manhunt*, which had already been banned in some countries. Stefan's father said, "The way Warren committed the murder is how the game is set out—killing people using weapons such as hammers and knives. There is some connection between the game and what he has done."

Industry response

A spokesman for the video games industry said, "simply being in someone's possession does not and should not lead to the conclusion that a game is responsible for these tragic events," and the police found no connection between the murder and *Manhunt*. Nevertheless, some retailers did remove the adult-rated game from their shelves.

"Youth violence in America has fallen dramatically over the precise time period that video games have skyrocketed."

Neil Seeman, Canadian lawyer and health care researcher

✖ "While video games may provide a simple excuse for the teenagers involved in this incident, responsibility for violent acts belongs to those who commit them."

Douglas Lowenstein, games industry spokesman, commenting on claims by teenage boys that they were acting out the Grand Theft Auto *game when they shot at passing vehicles in Tennessee*

✖ "I've played the *Mortal Kombat* game—you know it's violent, but it's sort of funny . . . the way they chop their heads off. You just laugh because you know it's not real."

16-year-old female respondent, Computer Games and Australians Today project

✿ STATISTICALLY SPEAKING

• One study has calculated that by the time typical American children reach the age of 18, they have seen 200,000 acts of violence and 40,000 murders on some sort of screen.

MORE TO THINK ABOUT

There is, as yet, no firm evidence that playing violent video games increases violent behavior. Many studies have found a link between the two, but this may be because those with existing aggressive tendencies are more likely to play violent video games.

Q: Can drunkenness ever be an excuse for crime?

MOST ADULTS who drink alcohol excessively do so without committing any sort of crime. However, it is accepted that there is a link between drunkenness and crime. Offenses ranging from anti-social behavior to dangerous driving, assault, and murder are more likely to occur where alcohol is involved. Defendants frequently argue that they were drunk and therefore not responsible for their own actions. However, others argue that drinking large amounts of alcohol is a choice, not an excuse.

Danish police remove a drunk man from a town center.

NO

"The statistics show a direct causal link between alcohol and the increase in reported violent crimes. Many people nowadays don't go out for a drink—they go out to get drunk."
Jan Berry, Chair of the Police Federation of England and Wales

X "Drinking and driving is a choice. It's a violent crime."
Millie Webb, victim of drunk driving and spokeswoman for Mothers Against Drunk Driving

X "[Drunkenness] should be viewed as an aggravating, not a mitigating circumstance. . . . A world in which having been a drunken member of an angry mob can protect against the legal consequences of murder is one in which we all have reason to feel profound unease."
Theodore Dalrymple, columnist

✓ YES

"While drunkenness is not normally an excuse or mitigating factor, where the abuse of alcohol . . . reflects the socio-economic circumstances and environment in which the offender has grown up, that can and should be taken into account as a mitigating factor."

Sentencing guidelines with regard to members of Aboriginal communities, Supreme Court of New South Wales

✓ "Alcohol brought the violence out of me."

Quote from a man who attacked his wife in Michigan

✓ "Malt beverages have an alcoholic content higher than that of most beers and lagers but with strong flavors like vanilla or lemonade. It is quite possible to drink such a product without realizing its true content."

Dr. Garry Slapper, Staffordshire University, U.K.

CASE STUDY

DRUNK DRIVING

Most countries prohibit driving at prescribed levels (measured as Blood Alcohol Content or BAC), but these levels vary by both country and situation. However, there is no foolproof guide to how much alcohol you can drink and still stay within the law. It depends on the type of alcohol you consume, how much you weigh, your sex, age, and metabolism.

Level at which a driver is legally intoxicated, by country:

Sweden: 0.02%

Australia: 0.05%

Netherlands: 0.05%

U.K.: 0.08%

U.S.: 0.08%

�֍ STATISTICALLY SPEAKING

• Those most likely to mix driving and alcohol are males ages 17 to 29.

�֍ STATISTICALLY SPEAKING

• Alcohol is present in more than 50 percent of all incidents of domestic violence, according to the U.S. Department of Health and Human Services.
• A survey in the U.K. found that 39 percent of "binge drinkers" (those who got very drunk at least once a month) age 18 to 24 reported committing an offense in the previous 12 months, compared to 14 percent of non-binge drinkers.

MORE TO THINK ABOUT

A French couple who allowed a drunken friend to drive home after a dinner party at their house were charged with being partially responsible for the car crash in which he killed himself and four others. They were acquitted (found not guilty). Was this a reasonable outcome, in your view?

FIND OUT MORE: www.madd.org www.alcoholconcern.org.uk
www.crimereduction.gov.uk/drugsalcohol8 www.drugwarfacts.org/alcohol.htm

Q: Are black people treated unfairly by the justice system?

MANY COUNTRIES with a mainly white population send a disproportionately high number of black people to prison. Black people also tend to be under-represented on juries, in the police force, and among lawyers and judges. Some argue that this is because the police are prejudiced or the courts are discriminatory. Others argue that black people are more likely to experience poverty or dislocation, which increases their likelihood of committing a crime.

YES

"Aboriginal people are grossly over-represented at all points of contact with the criminal justice system (except in regard to staffing and access to victim services, wherein they are grossly under-represented)."
Western Australian Aboriginal Justice Agreement

"'Are we impartial here?' is a question that arises when a person of color looks across the courtroom to see an all-white jury."
Pennsylvania Supreme Court Committee Report on Racial and Gender Bias in the Justice System

"Racial discrimination in the contemporary U.S. legal system remains deeply ingrained."
Amnesty International

�STATISTICALLY SPEAKING

- Out of 714,000 stops and searches by U.K. police in 2002, 12 percent were of black people, who make up 1.8 percent of the total population.

NO

"I don't see it."
The response of Rhode Island Supreme Court Chief Justice Frank Williams when asked if there was any racial discrimination in U.S. State courts

"I'm a police officer and all I'm trying to do is a good job and prevent crime. I get sick of hearing people complain when I stop them that it's because they're black and I have no reason to."
Clive, BBC Online "Talking Point"

✣ STATISTICALLY SPEAKING

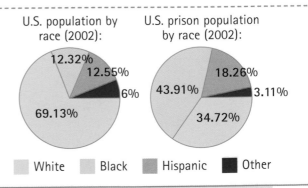

U.S. population by race (2002):
- 12.32%
- 12.55%
- 6%
- 69.13%

U.S. prison population by race (2002):
- 18.26%
- 3.11%
- 43.91%
- 34.72%

White Black Hispanic Other

STEPHEN LAWRENCE

Stephen Lawrence was murdered in London in 1993. No one has been convicted of his murder, but his parents and many activists believe he was the victim of a racist attack.

Doreen Lawrence, Stephen's mother, said, "My son was stereotyped by the police: he was black, then he must be a criminal. [His] crime was that he was walking down the road looking for a bus to take him home. Our crime is living in a country where the justice system supports racist murderers against innocent people."

After the murder, many people accused London's police force of ineptitude, complacency, and even racism in the way they conducted the investigation. A public inquiry was held in 1998, and the report concluded that the treatment of the Lawrence family and the police investigation itself were marred by "institutional racism" within the police force.

Nevertheless, the report also said, "We have heard no evidence of overt racism or discrimination [within the police], unless it can be said that the use of inappropriate expressions such as 'colored' or 'negro' fall into that category."

✱ STATISTICALLY SPEAKING

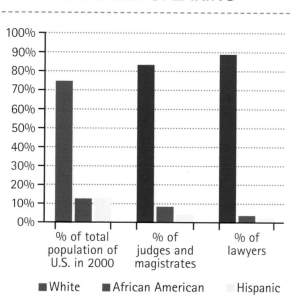

Bar chart legend: ■ White ■ African American Hispanic

Categories (x-axis): % of total population of U.S. in 2000; % of judges and magistrates; % of lawyers

MORE TO THINK ABOUT

The Canadian Criminal Code directs judges to consider non-custodial sentences wherever possible, "with particular attention to the circumstances of aboriginal offenders." Is it appropriate to use positive discrimination, also known as "affirmative action," to try to reverse the high proportion of aboriginal or black inmates in our prisons today?

FIND OUT MORE: www.buildingblocksforyouth.org www.cre.gov.uk
www.racismnoway.com.au www.affirmativeaction.org

Q: Should drugs be legalized?

Two drug dealers are caught selling cocaine by a hidden police camera.

IN MOST countries, the possession or sale of drugs such as marijuana, cocaine, and heroin is a criminal offense. Many believe that legalization would lead to an increase in addiction. However, others argue that the "war on drugs" is not working. They say that illegal drugs encourage smugglers and dealers, while addicts are forced into crime to pay for their habit. Marijuana is the most widely used illegal drug, but, unlike "hard" drugs such as heroin, it is not physically addictive. For this reason, some activists believe marijuana alone should be legalized, enabling police to focus on more "serious" crimes.

YES

✓ "The drug war is unwinnable, costly, and counterproductive. . . . Colombia saw a dramatic increase in violence and corruption as prohibition made cocaine a profitable commodity."

Sir Keith Morris, former U.K. ambassador to Colombia

✓ "If there had been a controlled environment for my son to take his heroin, and it had been supplied legally, he would still be alive."

Fulton Gillespie, whose son died after taking heroin that contained impurities

✓ "Drug prohibition turns otherwise law-abiding citizens into criminals and fuels crime at all levels."

Transform Drug Policy Foundation

✳ STATISTICALLY SPEAKING

• "Treatment has been shown to be 7.3 times more effective than law enforcement in reducing the drug problem and related problems such as crime."

Australian activist group Families and Friends for Drug Law Reform

NO "The legalization of drugs would make harmful and addictive substances affordable, available, convenient, and marketable. It would expand the use of drugs . . . and remove the social stigma attached to illegal drug use."

Drug Watch International

"To discourage the use of illegal drugs and to deter the damaging personal and economic effects of all types of drug use, individuals convicted of illegal drug offenses should be punished to the fullest extent prescribed by law."

George W. Bush, U.S. President

"The state must not assist its most vulnerable citizens to alienate themselves from society and ruin their lives."

Catholic Archbishop Giuseppe Lazzarotto, speaking against the legalization of drugs

"We'd make sure the drug traffickers have only two places to stay—jail or the cemetery."

Thaksin Shinawatra, Prime Minister of Thailand

CONFLICTING EVIDENCE?

"There are very few young heroin addicts in the Netherlands, largely thanks to the policy of separating the user markets for hard and soft drugs. The number of addicts . . . has been stable for many years."

Netherlands Ministry of Justice

----------------------⬇----------------------

"Since the legalization of marijuana in the Netherlands, heroin addiction levels have tripled."

U.S. Drug Enforcement Agency

✪ STATISTICALLY SPEAKING

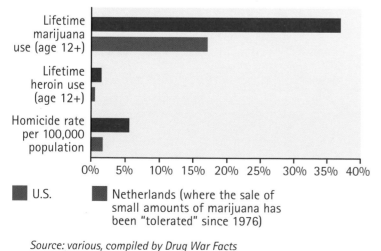

A comparison of drugs and violence in the U.S. and the Netherlands in one year

■ U.S. ■ Netherlands (where the sale of small amounts of marijuana has been "tolerated" since 1976)

Source: various, compiled by Drug War Facts

MORE TO THINK ABOUT
The debate about drugs involves a number of issues not covered here. These include: the costs to society of enforcing drug laws, civil liberties, alcohol and nicotine as legal drugs, and whether marijuana has any health benefits, particularly for sufferers of multiple sclerosis.

Q: Is downloading music from the internet the same as shoplifting?

MOST MUSIC, movies, and books are protected by copyright. This means that their creators, or "owners," have exclusive rights to copy and communicate their works to the public. Despite such laws, the music industry sees a growing threat from individuals who download music from unauthorized sites on the Internet. Because the copyright owner is not paid, many argue that this is the same as theft. However, others believe that copyright is an outdated law, and that unrestricted downloading benefits everyone, including the music industry.

NO "Researchers believe that most downloading is done by teens and college kids, groups that are 'money-poor but time-rich', meaning they wouldn't have bought the songs they downloaded. In that sense, the music industry can't claim those downloads as lost sales."

Sean Silverthorne, Editor, Harvard Business School journal

"The Internet is just one huge word of mouth. The more an artist is heard, the more likely people will go out and purchase the album legally."

High school student, Port Washington, New York

"The culture has shifted. It's not about buying music anymore. If the industry doesn't respond quickly, it's going to be in big trouble. We can't shut these people down."

Russell Simmons, co-founder of Def Jam Records

✔✔YES

"It's the same thing as going into a CD store and stealing the CD."
Britney Spears, singer

If you copy or distribute copyrighted music without permission, you can be prosecuted in a criminal court and sued for damages in a civil court.

✔ "Most songwriters are not rich or famous. They are hardworking craftsmen who depend on their royalties to provide for their children. Stealing music is stealing from their families."
Matraca Berg, songwriter

✔ "Whatever any of us feel about the price of anything, that doesn't justify stealing. Illegal file-sharing is theft under copyright law."
David Munns, vice-chairman of EMI Music

❋ STATISTICALLY SPEAKING

Percentage of Australia's population who agree that downloading unauthorized music from the Internet is like stealing from a record store

General population — 49%
Those under 25 — 33%

(Source: 2003 survey for the Australian Record Industry Association)

CONFLICTING EVIDENCE?

Among Internet-connected music consumers, those who say they are downloading more also say they are purchasing less by a margin of more than two to one.
Recording Industry Association of America

⬇

A study comparing music downloads with album sales showed that while the number of illegal downloads continued to increase, so did music sales.
Professor Felix Oberholzer-Gee and Koleman Strumpf

MORE TO THINK ABOUT

It is perfectly legal to download music from sites authorized by the owners of the copyrighted music, whether or not such sites charge a fee. It is illegal to download music from unauthorized sites or file-sharing "peer-to-peer" systems. It is also illegal to make unauthorized copies of music available to others through file sharing or CD burning. However, if you are unsure of the law, check first.

FIND OUT MORE: www.musicunited.org www.bpi.co.uk
www.pro-music.org www.fact-uk.org.uk

Q: Should victims' rights be more important than defendants' rights?

MANY PEOPLE believe that the justice system is unfairly weighted in the defendant's favor. Victims of crime often feel overlooked by the courts, and some think that a defendant's previous convictions should be made known to the jury to keep guilty people from walking free. However, the principle of "innocent until proven guilty" is enshrined in the justice systems of many countries, and the courts have to be extremely careful not to prejudice the outcome of trials.

YES

"Far too many of the nearly 25 million Americans who become victims of crime each year must struggle on their own with the enormous emotional, financial, and physical consequences of crime. . . . We must do more than merely tinker with offender-oriented systems that are not designed to address victims' needs."

Susan Herman, National Center for Victims of Crime

✔ "This measure . . . is designed to make it clear we are not going to have people playing the system and getting away with criminal offenses that cause real misery to ordinary citizens."

British Prime Minister Tony Blair, talking about a change in the law to allow juries to hear about a defendant's previous convictions

✔ "The victim impact statement is your opportunity to tell the court about the impact the crime has had on you. It is a factor that the court will take into account in sentencing. It may help the defendant realize the effects of what he or she has done."

Government of South Australia

NO

"Telling juries about [previous convictions] may get the result the government wants —more convictions—but far too many of them will be the wrongful convictions of innocent people."

John Wadham, director of the human rights organization Liberty

✖ "Society must separate contempt for his act from respect for his right."

The Israeli Supreme Court, upholding the right of prisoners to vote

✖ "Everyone charged with a penal offense has the right to be presumed innocent until proven guilty according to law in a public trial at which he has all the guarantees necessary for his defense."

Article 11, UN Declaration of Human Rights

CASE STUDY

RESTORATIVE JUSTICE

"Restorative justice" is the name given to the process of repairing the harm caused by crime. Victims, offenders, and affected members of the community are brought together by a court-appointed mediator. The idea is that offenders recognize the impact of what they have done and make amends, and victims have their harm or loss acknowledged. It is not generally intended as a substitute for punishment.

Results

Some studies report high levels of satisfaction with the process, but figures for the re-offending rates of participants are scarce, and it does depend on the offender pleading guilty before the process can begin. A U.K. Home Office report in 2005 found that "restorative cautioning," in which offenders apologize to their victims, had little effect on reconviction rates.

Damian Divine (left), a reformed offender, said his outlook had changed since he was faced with the parents of his 15-year-old victim. He said, "From my point of view, bringing the parents around made me realize that it had an effect on someone."

✸ STATISTICALLY SPEAKING

• More than 50,000 people in the U.K. are imprisoned each year awaiting trial. When they finally stand trial, one in five are acquitted (not guilty).

Source: Prison Reform Trust

- -

An ICM poll in the U.K. asked members of the public whether they thought a jury should know about a defendant's previous criminal record before they consider their verdict

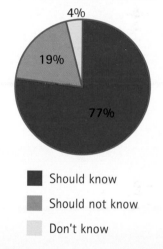

4%

19%

77%

■ Should know

■ Should not know

□ Don't know

MORE TO THINK ABOUT

There are many issues to consider when trying to balance the rights of the victim and the defendant that have not been mentioned here. These include: compensation for victims, early release of offenders from prison, and terrorist suspects imprisoned indefinitely without trial.

FIND OUT MORE: www.ncvc.org   www.innocentuntilprovenguilty.com
www.restorativejustice.org   www.voc.sa.gov.au   www.liberty-human-rights.org.uk

Q: Should euthanasia be treated as unlawful killing?

"VOLUNTARY EUTHANASIA" means receiving help in order to die. This "help" may mean supplying drugs, administering a lethal injection, giving information about how the drugs might be obtained, or not intervening to prevent such a death. In most countries, euthanasia is treated as unlawful killing, or even murder. However, in the Netherlands, Belgium, and the U.S. state of Oregon, "assisted suicide" for people who are terminally ill is legal in some circumstances.

YES

"If you see someone standing on a bridge considering suicide, you don't push them off. Euthanasia is giving them that push."

Spokeswoman for the Pro-Life Alliance

"Once the power to kill is bestowed on physicians . . . a patient can no longer be sure what role the doctor will play—healer or killer."

International Task Force on Euthanasia and Assisted Suicide

"[Euthanasia could] potentially create an open season for the killing of disabled people."

Tara Flood, U.K. Disability Awareness in Action

 NO

"This is the trial of everyone who's ever made a promise that they would help someone die gently if necessary, and the trial of every doctor who has helped and remained silent."

Lesley Martin speaking at her trial in New Zealand. Martin had given her terminally ill mother an overdose of morphine. She was convicted of attempted murder and jailed for 15 months

"The patient always makes the last act—swallowing the drug or opening a valve of a drip himself—so we never had a problem with the police."

Ludwig Minelli, director of Dignitas, a Swiss charity that helps terminally ill people die

"The law produces the apparently irrational result that people can choose to die lingering deaths by refusing treatment that keeps them alive . . . but they cannot choose a quick, painless death that their doctors could easily provide."

Professor Ronald Dworkin, University College, London

✺ STATISTICALLY SPEAKING

• A poll of disabled people in the U.K. found that 80 percent would back a bill allowing a rational disabled person with a terminal disease to be helped to die.

CONFLICTING EVIDENCE?

Does legislation mean more deaths?

According to law in the Netherlands, doctors involved in voluntary euthanasia must:
• be convinced that the patient's request is voluntary, well-considered, and lasting;
• be convinced that the patient's suffering is unbearable and unremitting;
• have reached the conclusion with the patient that there is no reasonable alternative.

Percentage of all deaths in Australia and the Netherlands, 1995

	Australia No legal euthanasia	Netherlands Limited euthanasia permitted
Voluntary euthanasia	1.7%	2.4%
Physician assisted suicide	0.1%	0.3%
Ending life without explicit request	3.5%	0.7%
Withholding life-prolonging treatment	28.6%	20.2%
Pain relief likely to hasten death	30.9%	19.1%
Total	64.8%	42.7%

In the Netherlands in 2001, it was estimated that doctors ended the lives of 840 people without their specific request. In a recent survey, 10 percent of Dutch senior citizens said they feared being killed by their doctor without their consent.

Dr. Jack Kevorkian was known as "Dr. Death" for his role in more than 100 assisted suicides. In 1999, he was convicted of second-degree murder for giving a lethal injection to a terminally ill patient who had requested it. He received a minimum 10-year prison sentence.

MORE TO THINK ABOUT

This debate has focused on the assisted deaths of older people who are terminally ill. However, the Netherlands is currently considering legalization on the assisted deaths of terminally ill babies and children and people who are mentally incapacitated. Is this the "slippery slope" that anti-euthanasia activists fear?

FIND OUT MORE: www.qrtl.org.au www.internationaltaskforce.org/holland.htm
www.ves.org.uk. www.euthanasia.com

Glossary

Aboriginal people who are native to a country—their ancestors have inhabited a region from the beginning.

Anti-social behavior defined by a wide range of problems such as noisy neighbors, graffiti, litter, and public nuisance.

Arson the criminal act of deliberately setting fire to something.

Biometric data any unique physical characteristic such as an iris scan or thumbprint by which a person can be identified.

Capital punishment the death penalty—the killing of a prisoner for a crime such as murder.

Copyright the law which gives exclusive rights to someone to copy and communicate his or her original works to the public.

Cyber crime crime conducted electronically via the Internet.

Death Row where prisoners who have been sentenced to death await execution.

Defendant person accused of a crime in court.

Delinquent a young person who has a tendency to commit crime.

Deprivation hardship such as homelessness or poverty.

Deterrent a punishment that acts as a warning to others.

Discrimination treating someone unfairly because he or she is different (e.g. of different color, sex, religion).

Download to transfer data, such as music, from a server, such as the Internet or host computer, to your own computer.

Euthanasia bringing about an easy death; assisted suicide.

Exclusion being barred because of bad behavior (e.g. from school).

Forensic chemical evidence such as DNA or soil particles that may be used in a court of law.

Heroin a highly-addictive illegal drug extracted from the Asian poppy.

Homicide unlawful killing.

Identity fraud use of the identity of a person without his or her consent, for a purpose of which the person is not aware, generally for an illegal activity, such as theft with credit cards.

Illegal immigrant someone who moves to another country without permission.

Impartial fair, without prejudice or favor.

Incarceration imprisonment.

Joy-rider person who has stolen a car in order to drive it for fun, probably recklessly.

Juror a member of the public who has been chosen to sit on a jury at a trial.

Juvenile a child or young person not yet an adult in the eyes of the law.

Legislation a law (or laws) that has been proposed or is already in force in a country.

Liberal someone who does not take a hard line, accepting a broad range of viewpoints.

Malt beverages drinks with a strong alcoholic base mixed with sweet or fruity flavors.

Marijuana a mood-altering drug from the cannabis plant, which is usually smoked. It is illegal in many countries.

Mentally incapacitated unable to make a rational decision or take responsibility for one's own actions.

Mitigating factor something that may lessen a person's responsibility for a crime (e.g. mental illness).

Non-custodial sentence punishment that does not involve a prison sentence (e.g. a community service order).

Offender someone who has been convicted of a crime.

Penal offense an offense punishable by law.

Prejudice a judgment formed beforehand or without knowledge of the facts; prejudice is sometimes an irrational suspicion or hatred of a particular group, race, or religion.

Premeditated an act that has been planned or considered beforehand.

Prohibition a law forbidding the sale of something such as drugs or alcohol.

Racism hatred of or prejudice against someone because of his or her race.

Rehabilitation help and support for offenders to stop them from re-offending.

Restorative justice a process in which an offender meets his or her victim to apologize or make amends.

Retroactively after the fact.

Terminally ill dying.

Terrorist someone who carries out a serious criminal act, often against innocent victims, to draw attention to his or her cause.

Unanimous in complete agreement.

Verdict the decision of a judge or jury at the end of a trial.

White-collar crime crime against business—often fraud or embezzlement.

Witness someone who sees an event and reports what happened, possibly in a court of law.

Zero tolerance the policy of pursuing every criminal, however small his or her crime.

Debating tips

WHAT IS DEBATING?

A debate is a structured argument. Two teams speak, one at a time, for or against a particular issue. Usually, each person is given a time limit, and any remarks from the opposing side are controlled. The subject of the debate is often already decided, so you may find yourself having to support opinions with which you might not agree. You may also have to argue as part of a team, being careful not to contradict what others on your side have said.

After both sides have had their say and had a chance to answer the opposition, the audience votes for the team it believes has made the strongest case.

DEBATING SKILLS

1 Know your subject

Research it as much as you can. The debates in this book give opinions as a starting point, but there are Web sites suggested that offer additional information. Use facts and information to support your points.

2 Make notes

Write down key words and phrases on cards. Try not to read a prepared speech. You might end up losing your way.

3 Watch the time

You may be given a set amount of time for your presentation, so stick to it.

4 Practice how you sound

Try to sound natural. Think about:
Speed—Speak clearly and steadily. Try to talk at a pace that is fast enough to sound intelligent and allows you time to say what you want, but slow enough to be understood.
Tone—Varying the tone of your voice will make you sound interesting.
Volume—Speak at a level at which everyone in the room can comfortably hear you. Shouting does not win debates. Variation of volume (particularly speaking more quietly at certain points) can help you to emphasize important points, but the audience must still be able to hear you.
Don't ramble—Short, clear sentences work well and are easier to understand.

GET INVOLVED—NATIONAL DEBATING LEAGUES

National Forensic League
www.nflonline.org

Debating Matters, U.K.
www.debatingmatters.com

American Forensic Association
www.americanforensics.org

Alberta Debate and Speech Association
www.compusmart.ab.ca/adebate/

Index

Acknowledgements

Picture credits: © Corbis Sygma: 21. © Lou Dematteis/Reuters/Corbis: 11. © Najlah Feanny/Corbis Saba: 22. © Brownie Harris/Corbis: 28. © Himmel Lizzie/Corbis: 12. © Reuters/Corbis: 6. © Fatih Saribas/Reuters/Corbis: 14. © Steve Starr/Corbis: cover, 27. © Pidgeon Thomas/Corbis Sygma: 43. © David Woods/Corbis: 24. Tim Ockenden/PA/Empics: 41. Laurence Cendrowicz/Franklin Watts: 25, 29. Chris Fairclough/Franklin Watts: 10. Rex Features: 4-5, 16, 18, 35. Francis Dean/Rex Features: 32. Isopress/Rex Features: 30. Mark St. George/Rex Features: 36. Keystone/TopFoto: 38-39. Novosti/TopFoto: 8.

Text credits: P6: 1 Vic Bilson, "Death in the School Yard": http://www.jeremiahproject.com/prophecy/schoolyard.html (07/01/05); 2 Anonymous, 2005; 3 Joschka Fischer quoted in "Cybercrime" by Peter Gould and Chris Summers, January 2001: http://news.bbc.co.uk/hi/english/static/in_depth/uk/2001/life_of_crime/cybercrime.stm (07/01/05). P7: 1 Don Weatherburn quoted in "NSW crime figures dip for a third year," Aug. 23, 2004: http://www.bananas-in-pyjamas.com.au/nsw/news/200408/s1182801.htm (07/01/05); 2 Rosemary Gartner, 1998 ; 3 Vincent Schiraldi, 1998. P8: 1 Richar Burr, "A Child On Death Row, A Tragedy Unfolding": http://www.ccadp.org/grahamchild.htm (07/01/05); 2 Daljeet Dagon quoted in "There are no silver spoons for children born into poverty," Barnado's, 2003: http://www.barnardos.org.uk/newsandevents/media/resource/REPORT.PDF (07/01/05); 3 Lisbet Palme, "No age of innocence: Justice for children," 1997: http://www.unicef.org/pon97/protec1b.htm (07/01/05). Page 9: 1 Dan quoted in "Is crime being tackled properly?" BBC online talking point, 2003: http://news.bbc.co.uk/1/hi/talking_point/3106369.stm (07/01/05); 2 Catholic bishops of New Zealand, "Creating New Hearts: Moving From Retributive to Restorative Justice," Aug. 30, 1995: http://www.ccjc.ca/currentissues/newzealand.cfm (07/01/05); 3 Haney, C., "The Social Context of Capital Murder: Social Histories and the Logic of Mitigation," *Santa Clara Law Review 547* quoting Decision, In the Matter of the Clemency Request of Robert Alton Harris, (Apr. 16, 1992). P10: 1 Nicole Billante, "The Beat Goes On: Policing for Crime Prevention," Center for Independent Studies, July 1, 2003; 2 Maureen Brookes quoted in *The Observer*, Nov. 27, 2004; 3 Sarah Teather quoted in *North West London Newspapers*, Nov. 3, 2004, 4 Slogan on Conservative Party campaign poster, U.K., 2005. P11: 1 Zaki Hashmi, BBC Talking Point, July 12, 2002: http://news.bbc.co.uk/1/low/talking_point/forum/2118682.stm (07/01/05); 2 Tim Anderson, "Zero tolerance" policing—a big lie," 1998: http://www.greenleft.org.au/back/1998/326/326p14b.htm (07/01/05). P12: 1 Stephen P. Bohrer quoted in *San Francisco Chronicle*, Dec. 1, 2001, 2 South Australia Department of Correctional Services, "Illicit Drugs and Correctional Services," June 2002; 3 Professor Paul Robinson quoted in *Penn News*, Apr. 22, 2004. P13: 1 Annabel Goldie, Press Release—Scottish Conservatives, Feb. 24, 2004; 2 U.S. Deputy Attorney General Larry Thompson—Press Release, Jan. 2003; 3 David Green quoted in *The Times* (London), May 12, 2004; 4 Levi's story: reproduced with permission of Prison Me No-Way!; P14: 1 David Blunkett, speech to Institute of Public Policy Research, Nov. 17, 2004; 2 Mrs. Jan Berry—Press release, Nov. 23, 2004; 3 Clive Williams quoted in *The Canberra Times*, Oct. 16, 2003. P15: 1 American Civil Liberties Union, 5 "Problems with National ID Cards," Sep. 8, 2003: http://www.aclu.org/News/NewsPrint.cfm?ID=13501&c=39 (07/01/05); 2 Adrian Beck from pamphlet "ID Cards: Arguments Against," *Liberty and Charter 88*, Dec. 2002; 3 Simon Davies, "In Search of Perfect Identity," *The International Privacy Bulletin*, Vol. 4, No. 2, spring 1996. P16: 1 Hu Jintao quoted in *Legal Daily*, May 4, 1996; 2 Vikki Haack quoted in "Many grieving families seek comfort and closure in the execution of the murderer. Do they find it?" *US News & World Report* , June 17, 1997; 3 John McAdams: prodeathpenalty.com (07/01/05). P17: 1 Amnesty: http://web.amnesty.org/library/index/engasa 170032004 (07/01/05); 2 Albert Pierrepoint, *Executioner: Pierrepoint*, Harrap, 1974; 3 U.S. Congress Subcommittee on Civil and Constitutional Rights, Staff report, 1993; 4 Hasham Dezhbakhsh, Paul H. Rubin and Joanna M. Shepherd, Emory University Paper, 2003. P18: 1 George W. Bush, State of the Union Address, Jan. 20, 2004; 2 Martin Narey quoted in *The Observer* (London), May 5, 2002; 3 UN High Commission for Human Rights, Standard Minimum Rules for the Treatment of Prisoners, first adopted in 1955. P9: 1 Peter Olohan, U.S. quoted in "Is prison the best punishment? Your reaction" BBC online Talking Point, Sep. 10, 1998: http://newswww.bbc.net.uk/1/hi/talking_point/168607.stm (7/4/05) 2 Matt Salmon, quoted in Klass Action Review, Fall 1998, Vol. 4, No. 3; 3 Wendy Utting. P20: YES 1 U.S. Constitution: Sixth Amendment; 2 Baroness Helena Kennedy, QC, "Law Reforms Show 'Disdain For Public'" by Lee Gordon, Camden New Journal, Nov. 21, 2002; 3 Robert D. Myers, Ronald S. Reinstein and Gordon M. Griller, Complex Scientific Evidence and the Jury, Judicature, Vol. 83(3), Nov.–Dec. 1999; NO 1 Lord Falconer, "Trial by Jury is it under threat": http://www.pcs.org.uk/Templates/Internal.asp?NodeID=884710 (4/7/05); 2 From court transcripts, Sacremento, California, Nov. 25, 1997; 3 Professor Richard Dawkins, "Three herring gull chicks . . . the reason juries don't work" *The Observer* (London), Nov. 16, 1997. P22: 1 Karen MacNutt, "Posted," Women & Guns: http://www.womenshooters.com/archive/old1103issue/macnutt 1103.html (7/4/05); 2 Second Amendment, U.S. Constitution; 3 Gary A. Mauser, "The Failed Experiment, Gun Control, and Public Safety in Canada, Australia, England, and Wales" *Public Policy Sources*, A. Fraser Institute Occasional Paper, Number 71 / Nov. 2003. P23: 1 National Rifle Association of America from FBI data: http://www.nraila.org/Issues/FactSheets/Read. aspx?ID=18 (7/4/05); 2 Transcript of John Howard interview With Philip Clark, Radio 2GB on Apr. 17 2002: http://www.pm.gov.au/news/interviews/2002/interview1600.htm (7/4/05); 3 Anne Pearson, 1996 4 Million Mom March: http://www.millionmommarch.org/about (01/07/05). P24: 1 James Douglas-Hamilton, Speech to Conference 2002: http://www.scottishtories.org.uk/conference/conf02-lordjd-h.html (07/01/05); 2 Grant Mcnally, Parliament of Canada: http://www.parl.gc.ca/37/2/parlbus/chambus/house/debates/049_2003-01-30/han049 _1835-E.htm (07/01/05); 3 Jeanette Basl, quoted on: http://www.crimevictimsunited.org/measure11/measure11argu ments.htm (07/01/05). P25: Judge David A. Young, Circuit Court for Baltimore City, Jun. 5, 1998, quoted in "Trying Children In Adult Courts" Human Rights Watch: http://www.hrw.org/reports/1999/maryland/Maryland-02.htm; 2 Barry Feld, quoted in "Adult crime, juvenile time" *Philadelphia Inquirer*, Mar. 14, 2004; 3 Lisbet Palme, "No age of innocence: Justice for children," UNICEF: http://www.unicef.org/pon97/protec1c.htm (07/04/05). P26: NO 1 Lisa Stevens, Jan. 9, 2003; 2 Ann Widdecombe, "Widdecombe: Together we can win war against crime," speech on May 22, 2001: http://www.conservatives.com/tile.do?def=news.story.page&obj_id=10538& speeches=1&type=print; (07/04/05); 3 Ron Lovelock, "Borstal changed my life," Oct. 17, 2002: http://news.bbc.co.uk/2/low/uk_news/2330061.stm (07/04/05); YES 1 Lord Bingham, giving evidence to the select committee on Home Affairs, Mar. 17, 1998; 2 The National Mental Health Association, "Juvenile Boot Camps": http://www.nmha.org/children/justjuv/bootcamp.cfm (07/04/05); 3 Lucie Russell, Press release from Smart Justice, July 29, 2003. P28: 1 Tasmania Police: www.police.tas.gov.au/police/police2001.nsf/W/Resources/CCAS -5GG8KL/?Open; 2 Essex police quoted in "Decoy cars will be first in the country," Kim Perks, May 16, 2002: http://213.210.6.88/crimedatabase/site/content.php?article_id= 339 (07/05/05); 3 Kevin Mills quoted in "Car Thefts Crackdown": http://www.southyorks.police.uk/ serving_you/ServingYouPg03SheffNorth.pdf (07/05/05); 4 Bob Hastings quoted in "Police urge better parenting after crash of joy-riding teens" by Jamie Berry, *The Age* (Australia), Aug. 15, 2003. P29: 1 William McCrea; 2 BBC online talking point, Sept. 2002, 3 Insurance Bureau of Canada: http://www.ibc.ca/ii_auto_theft_8.asp. P30: 1 Craig A. Anderson, "Violent Video Games: Myths, Facts, and Unanswered Questions," *Psychological Science Agenda*, Volume 16: No. 5, Oct. 2003; 2 Mary Lou Dickerson, Washington State Department of Health Press Release, 2000; 3 Barbara Biggins, ABC TV, Sept. 16, 2003. P31: 1 Neil Seeman, "In Defense of Video Games," CANSTATS, March 8 2004: http://www.canstats.org/readmore.asp?sNav=pb&id=640 (07/05/05); 2 Douglas Lowenstein quoted in "Video games back in U.S. dock" by Rachel Clarke, BBC News online, Sept. 15, 2003: http://news.bbc.co.uk/1/hi/technology/3104892.stm (07/05/05); 3 Computer Games and Australians Today Project, Office of Film and Literature Classification, December 1997. P32: 1 "Crime Stats Show That Government Must Tackle Binge Drinking," July 21 2004: http://www.polfed.org/FinalCS.pdf; 2 Millie Webb, spokeswoman for MADD: www.madd.org; 3 Theodore Dalrymple, City Journal, May 2, 2003. P33: Mr. Justice Wood, quoted in "Sentencing Aboriginal Offenders," 1992: www.legalaid.nsw.gov.au/data/portal/00000005/public/16163001099456570562.doc (07/05/05); 2 Quoted in: http://csswashtenaw.org/ada/resources/community/poster_words.html (07/05/05); 3 Dr. Garry Slapper, *Times Newspapers*, 2003: http://www.ias.org.uk/publications/alert/97issue1/alert9701_p6b.html (07/05/05). P34: YES 1 Western Australian Aboriginal Justice Agreement, Mar. 2004; 2 Pennsylvania Supreme Court Committee Report on Racial and Gender Bias in the Justice System, 2002; 3 Amnesty International: http://www.amnesty.ca/usa/racism.php (07/05/05); NO 1 Justice Frank Williams quoted in "No Racial Discrimination in RI Courts, Chief Justice Says:" http://www.insidepolitics.org/heard/heard081201.html (07/05/05); 2 BBC online talking point, Jun. 2002. P36: 1 Sir Keith Morris quoted in *The Guardian* (London), July 4, 2001; 2 Fulton Gillespie, speaking to Home Affairs Select Committee on Drugs, May 2002, 3 Transform Drug Policy Foundation, June 2004 briefing. P37: Drug Watch International: http://www.drugwatch.org/T&L%20Drug%20Legalization.htm (07/05/05); 2 "Responses Of President George W. Bush," Joint Center for Political and Economic Studies, 2004: http://www.jointcenter.org/2004election/Presidential-Survey-Bush-Response.pdf (07/05/05); 3 *The Observer* (London), Feb. 2005; 4 Thaksin Shinawatra, Mar. 24, 2003 quoted on: http://t2web.amnesty.r3h.net:80/pages/tha-010304-action-eng (07/05/05). P38: 1 Sean Silverthorne, "Music Downloads: Pirates—or Customers?" Jun. 21, 2004: http://hbswk.hbs.edu/item.jhtml?id=4206&t=innovation (07/05/05); May 2, 2002, © David Strom, Inc: http://www.strom.com/awards/287.html (07/05/05); Russell Simmons, Cyberposium 2003 conference, Jan. 18, 2003. P39: 1 Britney Spears, quoted in "Britney, Nelly, Missy Elliott Want You To Quit Stealing Music," Sept. 26, 2002: http://www.mtv.com/news/articles/1457802/20020926 /spears_britney.jhtml (07/05/05); 2 Matraca Berg, Music United 2003; 3 David Munns quoted in "EMI boss defends music industry; Universal drops prices," The Daily Roxette, September 4, 2003: http://www.dailyroxette.com/article. php/1375; 5 Recording Industry Association of America: http://www.riaa.com/news/newsletter/082602.asp (07/05/05); 6 Professor Felix Oberholzer-Gee and Koleman Strumpf, "The Effect of File Sharing on Record Sales," Mar. 2004. P40: YES 1 Susan Herman, Press release about parallel justice project, Oct. 30, 2003; 2 Tony Blair, Press Conference, Oct. 25, 2004; 3 Government of South Australia, 2001 © Attorney-General's Dept; NO 1 John Wadham, BBC News, September 2003 2 Israeli Supreme Court, 1996; 3 Article 11, UN Declaration of Human Rights. P42 NO: 1 Lesley Martin quoted in "To help someone die gently," Mar. 31, 2004: http://www.news24.com/News24/World/News/0,,2-10-1462_1506038,00.html; 2 Ludwig Minelli on BBC "Newsnight," 2002; 3 Ronald Dworkin, Life's Dominion—An Argument About Abortion and Euthanasia, Harper Collins, 1993; YES 1 Pro-Life Alliance, *The Observer* (London), December 5, 2004; 2 International Task Force on Euthanasia and Assisted Suicide © 1996–2004; 3 Tara Flood, speaking to the parliamentary select committee, 2004